Dealing with Difficult People

By Rhonda Scharf, CSP

Contents

Chapter 1: A Difficult Person Defined

It is so easy to feel that we run into difficult people everywhere we turn. Some days we feel as if the world is ganging up on us. We run across the person on the highway that deliberately rides our bumper, the person on the bus that has loud personal telephone conversations for everyone to hear, and that someone in the office who seems to think that it is just fine for them to eat a lunch they did not bring into the office!

And, let's be honest, some days we feel like our face is on a target and everywhere we turn, everyone is taking aim.

Those days, hours and situations can be draining. We can feel like the light at the end of the tunnel is a train coming straight for us. It makes going to work a chore sometimes not worth doing, and certainly affects our sleep, our stress and eventually our sanity.

This book is your hope. The hope that with the right skills you can deal with those difficult situations. The hope that you can overcome those days that break us down into a blubbering mess and the hope that someday those difficult people will just leave us alone.

We'll explore exactly how to create your strategy to deal with your difficult person and by the end of this book you'll have the confidence you need to face those challenging situations head on, without cowering away, and with the professionalism to make sleep at night easy.

Dictionary.com defines difficult people as those people who continually and chronically get in your way of you doing your job and living your life effectively.

That means it's not just on Fridays, it's not just when they're in a cranky mood, it's not just when they've got you in their targets, it's every single time. It's almost as if they go home and plot how to ruin your next day. Of course they don't, but it sure feels like that doesn't it?

Now according to some experts, that's only 2% of the population. That is a really small percentage which I don't happen to agree with. Because we live in an age where so much communication is done virtually, I believe that not only is that number much higher, but that it is rising exponentially daily. There is so much communication done on email, message boards, text, Facebook, etc., and people can be incredibly difficult and mean when they aren't face-to-face with the person they are attacking. You also know that if your job requires you to deal with people over the telephone, your average will be higher than 2% as well. Once you take away the human connection, people tend to be far more difficult than when they are face-to-face. For some it is a license to be difficult.

That being said, working with someone who continually and chronically gets in your way isn't as common as we think it is. They can be difficult at times, just not all the time. They can be swayed by bad moods, jealousy or sometimes you are in the wrong place at the wrong time. They don't fall into the technical definition of difficult people, they aren't difficult really, instead it is conflict you are dealing with.

Conflict

Let's go back to the dictionary for a moment, where we see that "conflict" is a state of being that occurs over a prolonged period during which issues are not addressed, thereby, adding to distance. (I often joke that sometimes when you look up a word in the dictionary you still don't know what it means!)

Conflict is *tension*. Most of the time, what people will refer to as dealing with difficult people is actually tension in a relationship. You might have had a really good friendship with somebody at one time, and then over time the little things start to get in your way. You think maybe they're sabotaging you and you call them difficult, but they're not really.

It's just more of a tension.

Now, the good news is the solution is pretty much the same for both of our situations, but it's good to recognize that it is actually fairly rare to be dealing with difficult people. Yes, they exist. There's no question that they exist, but most of the time it's tension and we have to learn to deal with that.

What we need is a strategy on how to work with this person, how to live with this person or to deal with what you perceive to be very difficult behaviour.

It's useful to know that if you identify someone as a difficult person, they will often see you as the difficult one! Difficult relationships are always two-way, and it's as if we get in each other's way. It feels deliberate too.

One person will block another person from doing something they need to do, or talk bad about them, or they'll say they're not capable of doing that thing and they won't give them any good assignments. Then the other person will do the same or similar thing back!

In my live program, **Dealing with Difficult People**, I do the following exercise that's usually an eye-opener for participants. Here's how that works.

1. I put them in pairs and ask them to imagine they are playing the childhood game of pattycake. Standing up and facing each other, they put their hands against their partners' hands.

2. In each pair there is a Partner A and a Partner B and we quickly assign roles.

I give the following instructions very quickly:

On the count of three, I want Partner A to push as hard as possible on Partner B. 1-2-3 Go!

Of course, Partner A pushes as hard as possible, which is exactly what I told them to do. Note, I don't tell Partner B what to do.

After just a few seconds I tell them to stop. Then I'll say, "Partner A, congratulations. You did what you're supposed to do. You've earned a raise. You followed instructions well and you're getting a promotion! Partner B, I didn't tell you what to do. What did you do?"

Now, you know that every single Partner B pushed back! It's an instinctive reaction that when somebody pushes, we feel threatened (literally and figuratively). We feel threatened and so we push back.

Here's how the conversation goes:

Me: So, Partner B, why did you push back? You weren't told to push back.

Partner B: It was instinctive I pushed automatically without thinking about it.

Me: Partner A, when Partner B pushed back, what did you do?

Partner A: I pushed harder.

Me: Partner A, you were trying to do your job and it seemed like Partner B was being difficult, right?

Partner A: Yeah, absolutely. They were stopping me from doing what I was trying to do.

Me: Partner B, why did you push back? Did Partner A seem difficult?

Partner B: Yeah, they were trying to knock me over.

Me: Partner A, were you trying to knock Partner B over?

Partner A: (*usually laughing*) No – just pushing hard. Not trying to hurt, just following instructions.

Me: Partner B wasn't Partner A just trying to do their job?

Partner B: Well, it didn't feel that way.

See how that happens? It's an automatic reaction that you push back. That doesn't make anyone a difficult person. When someone is literally or figuratively pushing, we push back. That's just reality.

Pushing feels like conflict. It felt like you were trying to knock me over. It felt like you were trying to stop me from doing my job. It felt like aggression; therefore, I reacted. In that situation, both Partner A and Partner B were difficult from each other's perspective. It's all in the perception.

Dealing with difficult people isn't about who is right and who is wrong; it is about changing the situation so we have no pushing happening (literally or figuratively).

So in order for us to develop the strategy that we need to deal with a difficult person, we have to realize quite clearly right from the start that we're part of the problem, and in order to be part of the solution, we have to get out of the way of the problem.

If you are dealing with a difficult person, you are still probably pushing back, but if you're dealing with tension, you're *definitely* pushing back—and you're creating more tension! The strategy we need is to not create more tension—it's to release that tension.

Chapter 2: Preparing to Build Your Strategy

You can't just say do *this* and it goes away; it's not just do *this* then they will leave you alone. It's never that simple. You need to formulate a strategy, and there are many steps to the process.

See It from Their Perspective

Let's say you are preparing to build your strategy for dealing with a person you've identified as difficult. Take a piece of paper and write on it, "I'd be more effective working with Jennifer or Bob if...." Now complete the sentence.

> I would be more effective
> working with _____
> If _____.

If you are like 99.9% of the folks in my audiences, the next word will be *she* or *he*. I'd be more effective working with Bob if *he* worked somewhere else! I'd be more effective working with Jennifer if *she* had a better attitude or if *she* didn't go over my head, if *she* let me do my job, if *she* would stop talking. We would always work better with someone if *they* would just follow the rules we've created.

Is that what you wrote? Okay, so you would be more effective working with someone else if they would do something else. But the reality is: *they* want *you* to do something else!

If they were reading this book, they would put your name in the difficult person's field and finish the sentence their own way. The very same way you blamed them, they would blame you!

Our strategy involves forcing ourselves to look at it from their perspective. How do they see you as being difficult? I know this is hard to do. A lot of people say, "I'm not difficult. I'm really easy to work with. I'm not the problem."

I'm not saying you're the problem or you're not the problem, but if you were the other person, what is the *perception* from their point of view of what you are doing? That's the first part of this strategy.

Imagine you are driving down the highway just slightly above the posted speed limit. What comes charging up behind you is a sports car, with those super bright halogen lights. They get within inches of your bumper and start to flash the lights to indicate they want you to move over so they can get past you.

What do you do?

I know, you lightly tap the breaks, you slow down, and sometimes some of you actually move over right?

So who is being difficult here?

From your perspective it is very clear the car behind you is being difficult. They are driving too quickly, they are endangering you by being too close to your bumper, and flashing their bright lights is just plain rude. From your perspective, they should just go around you and get out of the way. They are clearly being difficult as you were just nicely driving down the highway.

So let's put our feet in their shoes and see what they see:

You are driving quickly, therefore in the outside left lane of the highway. As you quickly approach the other car, you realize you are going much faster than they are, and want to alert them that you are here so they can easily slide to the adjacent lane allowing you access to pass. You aren't trying to be rude, you aren't being disrespectful, but you are calmly saying, "Just in case you didn't notice, I'm here and I'd like to pass. Please move to the other lane so I can pass you legally and safely."

But what happens when you do that? They deliberately tap their breaks. They deliberately slow down. They've proclaimed themselves the self-appointed police officer and have decided that you are driving too quickly, and it is their job to slow you down.

Looking at it from both perspectives, who is being difficult here?

In the first situation, it is the person in the rear being difficult, and in the second, it is the person in the lead being difficult.

It isn't about right or wrong; it is about seeing the behaviour from both perspectives, as that is important for our strategy. If you get stuck on who is right and who is wrong, you are clearly part of the problem.

As we prepare our strategy, make sure you have taken the time to see how your behaviour is being seen as difficult.

> Reading between the lines here, go back to your statement, "I would be more effective working with Jennifer if x" and write it again from Jennifer's perspective.

This will help you create the strategy you need to deal with difficult people. If you don't look at it from the other perspective, you are potentially creating more tension, potentially being too stubborn, and potentially being very difficult back. Don't be the reason someone else has to buy this book!

Sometimes when you do this, your tension disappears immediately and your situation is solved. For our highway analogy, if you are the type of person to automatically move over when someone is in your rear view mirror, then you have alleviated the tension by just moving over. It certainly doesn't affect your driving trip at all, so why tap the breaks and potentially endanger yourself? Why slow down just to annoy the other person? It doesn't make sense to antagonize at 70mph.

The same is true with our Partner A and Partner B activity. Every once in a while I will have a Partner B who doesn't push back. They allow Partner A to push as hard as they can. When that happens, almost every time, Partner A stops pushing very quickly. Since it wasn't the goal of Partner A to knock Partner B over, they stop pushing before anyone falls over. They did what they were supposed to do, and they stop immediately.

No tension that way at all.

Sometimes when we realize that we are part of the problem, and we immediately stop being part of the problem, the tension goes away. By being honest with ourselves we can get out of the way and the situation dissipates quickly and naturally.

Don't interpret that as always allowing the difficult person to have their way because it is easier. That is what has taught some people to be difficult — the whole "the squeaky wheel gets the oil" saying.

When I'm Partner B, there is no difference to me if my hands are 12 inches in front of me, or 4 inches in front of me. However, it does matter to me if you are still pushing me at 1 inch away from me. You've crossed a boundary. In this situation it is a personal space boundary and I'm pretty certain that you are trying to knock me over, and I do need to protect my space and safety.

I can offer resistance once you've hit my boundary mark. I won't necessarily push you all the way back, but I'm going to stop you once you've hit my boundary.

We talk more about boundaries in Chapter Six.

Chapter 3: What is Their Payoff? Why Are They Doing This?

Sometimes getting out of the way isn't the right answer (because of boundaries, rules or other reasons), and it doesn't always work even when you do that. Since dealing with difficult people is more than just not being part of the problem, we need to create a strategy that will allow us to deal with the difficult behaviour.

The first part of the strategy is to ask yourself why they are doing this. What is the payoff for them? What do they get from this behaviour? All behaviours in life are caused because we get something from them.

I have a cup of tea because it soothes me. I have dinner because it gets rid of the tummy grumbling. I go for a nap because it makes me feel good when I'm well rested. I like to go to the beach and feel good. Whatever it is, there is always something I get for it. I drive fast on the highway because it gets me there faster and I don't have extra time to waste. There's always a payoff to behaviour.

When you look at the "I'd be more effective working with Jennifer if..." statement, what is Jennifer's payoff? What do you think she is getting from the difficult behaviour you perceive?

Let's look at a couple of examples:

I would be more effective working with Jennifer if she would just stop talking too much and be more positive about life.

I perceive that she talks too much, she never shuts up, it's always negative, it's too hot, it's too cold, it's too brown, it's too white, it's too green, it's too wet or it's too dry! She's a chronic complainer.

To someone who is a positive thinker, this constant negativity can easily be seen as difficult behaviour. It feels as if she knows you would prefer to work in quiet and that she is trying to get you in a bad mood by pointing out all the negativity about anything and everything.

Why is she doing that? Why is she constantly whining about something? What is her payoff?

The payoff for her is attention. She just wants someone to talk to. She probably isn't trying to drive you insane, she is just much more verbal than you, and likes the attention that having a conversation brings her. She has learned that being chatty encourages others to join in the conversation, or listen to her. She doesn't want to be quiet and invisible, she wants attention.

People learn at a very young age that any attention is better than no attention. That's why kids act out at school because it's about attention, right? Think about the payoff she is getting. She just wants someone to talk to and over the years has learned that one of the ways to get people to join in the conversation, or listen to it, is to be negative.

Isn't that how our world is designed? We don't report news on all the good things that happen during the day, we report on the bad. Major weather bulletins are about impending storms and chaos, not a picture perfect day. Celebrities know that bad publicity is better than no publicity. It's the same thing on a smaller scale.

I grew up in the small town outside of Ottawa, I mean a really small, itty bitty town and a farming community. I was a totally middle-of-the-road, middle class, small town girl. I didn't grow up on a golf course, but I don't think my dad knew that because my dad was extremely picky about the way his grass was cut. He had an exact way that you cut the grass so that it looked like a golf course. It was 45 degrees one week and then next week it was the other

25

45 degrees. Apparently, according to Dad, that made the grass grow better! He was really worried about his grass.

Tina is my stepsister, and she's ten years younger than I am. By the time she came to live with Dad and Dad's wife, Sharon, I was already an adult and out of the house.

Dad decided that at 13 Tina was old enough to learn to start cutting the grass. Being a typical teenager, Tina didn't want to cut the grass. But you have to understand, Dad doesn't ask you to do things. Dad tells you to do things, so you're cutting the grass. He says to Tina, "Come on, I'm going to show you how to cut the grass." He shows her how to cut the grass in those 45-degree angles, and she doesn't want to do it. But she knows she has no choice.

The week goes by and it's her turn to cut the grass. She goes out and cuts the grass, but how does she cut it? Dad's 45-degree angles? No. She cuts it in circles. She must have cut every blade of grass 8 times. It's cut alright, but when Dad pulls into the driveway and sees his newly mowed lawn, he is not pleased! "Oh, my God! What will the neighbors think? The grass being cut like that, what a disgrace!"

Naturally, he yells and screams at Tina and he says, "Come on out here. I'm going to show you how to cut the grass properly." He goes out and shows her how to cut the grass again.

Tina still doesn't want to cut the grass. Hardly any fun for a 13 year old. The next week when she has to cut the grass again how does she cut the grass? In circles.

That was the last time Tina ever cut the grass. She was far smarter than I ever was as a teenager.

Let's look at this story from Dad's perspective. Tina has, very deliberately from his perspective, completed the task wrongly. She was being difficult. He knew she didn't want to cut the grass. She was only doing it because she had no choice in the matter. From his perspective, she was doing it wrong just to spite him, and to get out of continuing the job because she knew how much it would frustrate him. She was certainly being difficult, and her payoff, from Dad's perspective, was that she gets out of doing the job because she knows he won't accept that. He can't have his grass cut like that, so she'll do it again and again until he can't handle it anymore. She's saying to herself, "Ha, got out of cutting the grass." If you were my dad, that is exactly how you would see Tina's behaviour.

Let's look at it from Tina's perspective because it is important to see things from both sides.

Dad is being difficult because he told her to cut the grass and she did and he still wasn't happy! Every blade of grass on that lawn was cut. He asked her to cut it and she did, and it still wasn't good enough. He's insisting it be done *his* way. That makes *him* difficult from her perspective. She thinks Dad is being a control freak.

Can you see Tina's perspective as well?

Whichever of the two roles you look at in that situation, you can see how the other person perceives the opposite to be difficult, and you can see what the potential payoff is for each.

Remember, it isn't about right or wrong. Whether you side with Dad or Tina in this situation is irrelevant. If we are going to solve this tension filled situation, we need to apply our strategy.

The first part of the strategy? What are they doing and what is the payoff? Why are they doing it?

Don't be too quick to remove the payoff for the other person. That's the instinct that had Partner B offering resistance to Partner A trying to do their job. Taking away the payoff is not necessarily the solution.

Tina is a perfect example of that. Insisting that she cut the grass her own way (thereby taking away Dad's need to have it cut his way, or his control), would probably backfire if Dad hadn't backed down and cut the grass himself. You can imagine that each week they would get into a terrible battle and the tension would be thick every time Dad saw how Tina cut the grass. If she insisted on taking away his control, and he continued to insist it be done the way he wanted would have escalated this situation exponentially.

Tina has to evaluate what taking away that payoff would do. Many times it is the wrong answer as it just increases the tension levels.

What about your attention seeker? What happens when you take away attention? They just try harder to get your attention. Have you ever seen a child throw a tantrum in a store? The ability to get attention is deeply ingrained in some people.

Your control freak? What happens when you try to take away their control? They panic and need even more control in other areas. Ever work for a micromanager? You know that trying to take away their control has hazardous results.

Other common payoffs include:

- the need to win
- the need to be the favourite (teacher's pet type of payoff)
- the need to be right
- the need for self-esteem (or even be better than everyone else)
- the need to be noticed (attention)
- the need to be heard
- the desire to get out of doing work (doing it wrong so you don't ask me again)

This list is by no means complete. Once you have figured out what the payoff is, the first step of your strategy is set.

The biggest payoff, of course, is control. In fact, we're all control freaks — just to different degrees.

When it comes to your job, your reputation, your life, how controlling are you? If somebody is potentially flirting around the edges of your reputation or the perception of how you do things, will the control freak in you not step forward and say, "No, don't do that"? Of course it will.

Ask yourself what would happen if you took that payoff away? What is likely to happen to their behaviour?

If you said, it would get worse, then you are on-the-right-track indeed!

Although it is the instinctive reaction to take away their payoff, the reality is that often that is the wrong approach. Clearly that is situational, so let's continue with our strategy to see what else we can do to lessen the tension or resolve the situation entirely.

Chapter 4: Is this Innocent or Intentional?

When I ask people to consider this question in my workshops, they often say, "What do you mean, innocent or intentional? Isn't it *always* intentional?"

It always *feels* intentional. For example, in my previous story, Tina would say that Dad was deliberately insisting it be done his way, so his behaviour was intentional. Dad is thinking Tina is deliberately cutting the grass wrong just to annoy him so she doesn't have to do it anymore. He would say her behaviour was intentional.

I'm willing to bet that Dad doesn't perceive *his* behaviour as being difficult, because according to the way my dad was raised, this is the way you cut grass. This is the right way to do it. Cutting it in circles is wrong. He's not being difficult. He's doing it correctly from his perspective.

If you take that example into the workplace, and you have someone who is constantly correcting you — pointing out what you did wrong, identifying to you every little mistake you have made, right down to little typos — it feels as if they're nitpicking constantly and, to you, that is being difficult.

The person above who is being nitpicked at would say, "Mary is constantly on my case. She points out every single thing that is wrong, including stupid little things that don't matter. She is being difficult. She is trying to make me look bad. She is trying to get me fired."

Whereas, Mary would say, "I'm trying to make you better. I'm trying to point out what you're doing wrong so that you don't do it wrong the next time. I'm trying to help you keep your job. I'm trying to help you do your job better." She wouldn't perceive her behaviour as difficult at all.

If I were to ask you if Mary is being difficult, innocently or intentionally, you would probably say, "Absolutely intentional. She's deliberately pointing out every single mistake that I make." It's intentional, but Mary doesn't see that as being difficult. She sees that as being helpful. Therefore, it's an innocent behaviour because she is completely unaware that behaviour bothers you. She isn't trying to be difficult.

Go back to our driving example:

You are driving on the highway, and I want come up behind you and want to pass you. I want to drive faster than you are going, so I need to be ahead of you.

So I get very close to your bumper and I flash my lights to say to you, "Please move over. I'd like to get by." Meanwhile you're in front of me, thinking, "Look at the jerk behind me flashing lights. Go around!" You're thinking I am deliberately being difficult, whereas, I don't think I'm being difficult at all. This is an innocent please-move-over-I'd-like-to-go-by flash.

Is your tapping the breaks and slowing down innocent or intentional? I'm pretty sure that is intentional as you are deliberately trying to take away what it is that I want (my payoff).

If you were a distracted driver and didn't realize I was there and panicked a bit when I flashed my lights, but quickly moved to the other lane, I would assume the tap on the breaks was innocent as you weren't trying to stop me from getting past you. You weren't trying to take away what I needed from the situation.

What is likely to happen if you do tap your breaks or slow down deliberately? I might react to your virtual pushing back and do something intentional right back. We have aggravated each other – each assuming the other was in the wrong. We have all seen road-rage happen. We have all seen two people get into a completely inappropriate and potentially dangerous situation because they are both being deliberately difficult to the other person.

Behaviour

I don't have to agree with their behaviour. I don't have to think it's right, but I need to be able to look at the behaviour in a completely different way, from a different perspective. Is there a possibility they don't realize their behaviour is being considered difficult?

Think back to the person who is chronically negative. Do they consider their behaviour difficult? No. Is their constant whining (your description, not theirs) innocent or intentional? It's actually innocent. They don't realize they're being negative. They're just making conversation.

They've learned that this kind of conversation gets a reaction. That reaction is attention, and that's what they want. When you go back to the list of payoffs we were talking about earlier, one of the payoffs is attention, and we see everyone else as competition for attention. Innocent or intentional? Do you think they actually think this through, or it is just who they are? It's almost always innocent.

If we go back to our list of payoffs and why people do what they do, most of the time, those payoffs are so engraved in someone's personality that their behaviour is innocent. It's not intentional. It's an innocent behaviour because they are unaware they are doing it, and unaware that it bothers you.

Dad needing the lawn cut on angles was innocent behaviour. He wasn't trying to be difficult, that was the way the grass needed to be cut from his perspective.

The first time Tina cut the grass? Innocent. She cut the grass. When that angered Dad and he showed her how he wanted it cut, and she cut it in circles *again*, that was intentional.

Dealing with Difficult People

Chapter 5: Our Choices

The next stage of our strategy is to decide which part of the equation you are going to change to get a different result.

Right now you both are acting and reacting to each other and the tension is rising. Neither the situation nor the tension is going away so continuing to do the same thing isn't going to get you a different result.

> The Definition of Insanity is doing the same thing over and over again and expecting different results.

People on both sides of the situation have a payoff and it's often a different payoff, which can easily escalate the tension.

To make matters worse we don't even realize what our own payoff is. Go back to the stage where we are setting up our strategy and be honest with yourself when putting your feet in the other shoes. Answer each step of our strategy from both perspectives. What payoff does the other person perceive you are getting, and is it innocent or intentional?

Many times, the reason we react the way we do is control. I think you're going to knock me over, so I'm going to stop you from knocking me over. I'm going to keep control.

Go back to Sue and Mary for a moment. Mary points out all of Sue's mistakes; a typo here, a mistake there, all the little things that annoy Sue by Mary's know-it-all attitude. Mary thinks she's being helpful to Sue. However, Sue is getting frustrated and angry at Mary pointing everything out, so she doesn't forward things to her, doesn't keep her in the loop. She's deliberately keeping Mary out of the loop because she doesn't want all her mistakes pointed out constantly.

Naturally, Mary sees that as difficult behavior. "Why is she not sending information to me? She's being very difficult." In fact, Sue's act of revenge is a form of control.

It really is a two-way situation (both perceiving the other person is being difficult) and unfortunately, at this point, everyone makes the decision that they have to "fix" the other person.

At the beginning of this book I asked you to complete the sentence, "I'd be more effective working with Jennifer if..." If the next word you add is 'he' or 'she', then you're trying to fix the other person. You're trying to get them to change.

There are three different areas that you may want to change in order to get a different result from any situation.

1. The system

Maybe Sue doesn't want to send all her work to Mary and the system needs to be changed so that Mary doesn't need to see everything. Perhaps you work in a very large organization where to get rid of a challenging personality or get rid of a difficult person is next to impossible. When I say "the system", I mean your company, your union, your government, your laws. It's a brutally difficult thing to change. It can be done though.

Have you ever watched the movie Erin Brockovich? The system can be changed, but it isn't easy, and it isn't quick. While it is one approach, I would not put all my eggs into that basket.

2. The other person

You're not going to change the other person. Period.

Understand that every morning, Mary wakes up in bed saying to herself, "Today Sue is going to do her job without mistakes. Today she is going to slow down, proof read and finally understand how important it is that we do things without errors. Today is her maturity day. Today she's going to figure it out."

And across town, Sue is lying in bed saying, "Today Mary is going to leave me alone. Today she'll stop picking on every little thing showing me how smart she is and trying to make me feel stupid and inferior. Today Mary is finally just going to focus on her own business, and leave mine alone."

Every morning we wake up hoping the other person is going to see the light and all of a sudden be wonderful to work with, but they are hoping you are going to do that too! The fact is you can't change another person.

At work your difficult person probably doesn't like you, so what is the incentive for them to do what you want them to do? In personal relationships we may even love the other person and we still can't (or won't) change for them.

Trying to change the other person is making you the difficult one as you are being stubborn. Find another way to ease the tension in the relationship or situation.

3. You

That leaves really the third prime target for change. The only person you can change is you. It's not about putting all the blame on you, but it's about taking responsibility for changing the way you do something.

Let's go back to our partners A and B in the pattycake game.

Remember, as Partner A pushes, Partner B naturally pushes back. But what if Partner B makes a change and offers no resistance, what happens then? The answer is that Partner A stops pushing very quickly, because there's no tension. So by making a change in her own behavior, Partner B has changed the situation.

So you're driving along the highway and I come up on your bumper and flash my lights.

If you just move over and let me by, that situation is done five seconds later. I'm gone. I'm not in your life. I'm not causing you difficulty, and you're not causing me difficulty. As a result, there's no tension and there's no road range. The situation is over because you chose to just move over.

Taking this back to the workplace now, if as Partner B, if I don't offer any resistance to you, that might mean I don't get in your way of you doing your job, then you simply do your job and stop what I see as your difficult behavior, and there's no tension.

Choose option 3 to get a different result. Change what YOU are doing.

Chapter 6: Boundaries

Let's talk for a moment about boundaries. There are boundaries in every situation, and as part of your strategy you need to know what your boundaries are. There is a middle space between the starting point of the other person's difficult behaviour and the boundary beyond which I will not tolerate it. In that middle space, that's where you can avoid resisting and see if the behaviour stops.

In our workplace situation between Sue and Mary, when Mary points out Sue's error, Sue's past response has been to say something along the lines of, "Why do you always point out my errors? Why do you always think you're better than me?" But what if Sue chooses to say instead, "Thank you for pointing that out, Mary"? Sue is still annoyed, because she really doesn't want Mary to point out her mistakes, but now Mary is no longer feeling threatened by that response, so the tension dissolves on her end. Mary is trying to help Sue, and if Sue doesn't push back and create tension, Mary may interpret Sue as understanding why Mary identified the mistakes instead of creating a new tension.

There are still boundaries. If Mary crosses over what Sue perceives to be a line, that's different.

For example, instead of pointing out the problem to Sue, Mary goes to Sue's boss about the mistakes instead. I'd say that's definitely crossing a boundary. It's one thing to point out I've made a mistake, it's another to report it to someone else. In that case, Sue might say, "Mary, if you have a problem with my work, I'd prefer you to come to me with it instead."

If someone crosses your boundaries, you must respond. You don't need to create tension outside those boundaries, because that causes needless drama for everyone and potentially making you the difficult person!

This comes back to our strategy. Figure out what the other person is doing, why they are doing it (their payoff) and whether you can live with it.

Let's assume their payoff is attention. Can you live with working with someone who constantly needs attention, realizing it's nothing to do with you but just his or her personality? If you can live with it and not take it personally, then live with it. Just get out of the way and the tension disappears. Stop pushing back.

I decided to do that with my boys when they were growing up. Their definition of clean and my definition of clean were completely different. I had boundaries, but why create tension if it is something I could live with? They were exhibiting some signs of independence and control, but I decided I could live with that, so I did. Within reason of course.

If you can't live with it, ask yourself whether it is innocent or intentional, and what can you do to get a different result? In the case of that chronically negative person, maybe you can live with their getting attention. What you can't live with is the negativity — that's a boundary for you.

Your solution, your strategy becomes, "Okay, I can live with the attention they need. I can't live with the negativity. What can I do to change the negativity?" Every time they say something negative, I'm going to say something positive. As soon as they say "Oh no, it's raining again" I'll say, "Oh well, it's good for the flowers." That becomes your strategy, realizing there are some things you can change and some things that you can't. By doing that, it also puts you a little bit more in control, and you get your payoff, which is blocking the negativity that you can't live with. So the situation gets a little easier for you to deal with.

Usually the immediate reaction when we're dealing with a difficult person is to take away their payoff. We say to ourselves, "I know this is what you want, and you're not going to get it!"

The instinctive reaction is to not let them have their payoff. This, of course, now makes *you* the difficult person because they need that control, they need that attention, they need that competitiveness, they need that ... whatever it is. By removing that, you're actually a very big block to what they need.

For example, I know that Ralph needs to be the center of attention. I'm not going to take that away from him. It's just not going to work. He needs it more than I need him not to have it. I can try to be the center of attention at work. I can try to be the teacher's pet or the boss's pet, but he needs that more than I do, so his behaviour is just going to get worse. For me to try to take that away from him, it's going to become a battle of wills. So the instinctive reaction is not always the effective one.

When you're planning your strategy, ask yourself, "Can I live with that? What is it I can't live with? What is my boundary and what can I do to change that?"

As soon as you start to change what you are doing, you get a different reaction from the other person, a different final result.

A word of warning here: you can expect that the difficult person's behavior will get worse before it gets better. That's because the rules changed, but they weren't told the rules just changed. Habit has them pushing back and you just did something different. Don't panic when this happens, it is actually a good sign.

There's a good analogy in the child in a grocery store example. Mom says, "If you behave while we're getting groceries, I'll get you a candy bar on the way out." (Yes, I know, we're not supposed to bribe, but let's face it, we do!)

Of course children typically don't like grocery stores, and it seems as if they never behave in grocery stores. By the time you get to the checkout, they've misbehaved and they say, "I want my candy bar." You say, "Oh no, you lost that on aisle two!" What does the child do? They yell. They cry. They misbehave. Their behaviour gets worse the longer you hold out. They'll have that tantrum in the grocery store we've all seen happen.

That behaviour may be the norm for many two-year-olds, however, we also see it in forty-year-olds because the same thing happens at work. They learn that if they just keep acting up, they'll get what they want. Remember Tina and the grass? She knew that as long as she kept cutting the grass in circles, she was eventually going to get out of the grass cutting. Those two-year-olds become teenagers, and then they come into our workplace. At work we have co-workers who deliberately do things wrong, ignore deadlines and have adult style tantrums because they are going to get what they want. They learned at a young age that to have an adult-style tantrum gives them the result they want in the end, and that final result is more important to them than the chaos it creates for others.

We all know someone at work we wouldn't give an important task to. We know that if we did, they would do it wrong, or not do it at all, causing us much more work in the end. They've taught us not to give them extra work. They don't want extra work, and their behaviour is reinforcing what they want. It works doesn't it? Their need to get out of extra work is more important than your taking a stand and letting an important task go undone because you are more concerned about your reputation than you are about sharing the work equitably.

The question is, isn't the payoff that they get their own way? Sometimes it is, and this is part of the reason why you have to look at what your own payoff is. Don't you want your own way too? Is there a happy medium for both?

Dealing with difficult people is not about *my way and not your way* — that's bullying. It's about finding the solution that works for both. I'm probably going to have to give up a bit and you're probably going to have to give up a bit. It's a grown-up concept known as compromise, and hopefully we are both willing to do that. It's unreasonable for me to think I can take away your payoff completely and get my entire payoff. That's completely unreasonable.

There is a compromise component to dealing

with difficult people, and when that's not achievable we are actually dealing with a bullying situation, because bullies are not willing to compromise. With bullies, the behavior is always intentional and they're not going to change. That's not tension in a relationship — that's a personality problem. But that's a subject for another book, so let's get back to just plain old difficult people!

Dealing with Difficult People

Chapter 7: What to Do When Nothing Has Worked So Far

Sometimes we feel we've tried everything and wonder what's left for us to try! Our strategy continues.....

First, look at the last five interactions that you've had with this person and evaluate from your strategy points:

- What is it that they did that you didn't like?
- What behaviour was it you're calling attention to?
- What was the payoff for them, in your perception?
- Was the behaviour innocent or intentional?

Next, view the situation from their perspective and answer those questions about you as *they* might see it. Not necessarily how you intended they see it, but how they *probably* perceived it.

- What is it that you did that they didn't like?
- What behaviour are they responding/reacting to?
- What is the payoff for you, from their perspective?

- Do they view your behaviour as innocent or intentional?

Also consider how you have reacted in the past to those issues. If I perceive that in the last five business meetings we've had, your tone towards me was very condescending and I feel you are treating me like an idiot, then what have I done in the past? What has been my response pattern? I need to recognize the pattern, because now I need to break that pattern by doing something different.

If I've been pushing back, clearly that hasn't worked, so now what can I do that will get a different response? Can I choose to say nothing at all? Can I choose to call you out on your behaviour? What behaviour of my own am I willing to change?

Having identified what you are going to do differently the next time that situation occurs, you still have to do the hard part! You need to stick with your new plan a minimum of five times. Even if it feels completely wrong, stick with it five times. No breaks in the middle, five consecutive times and then at the end of those five times, evaluate. Is it getting better?

Is it getting worse? You can expect their behaviour is probably going to get worse before it gets better, so that's why we need to wait at least five times before evaluating. You can also expect it is going to feel uncomfortable for you (but hopefully the thought of doing nothing different and allowing the situation to continue is uncomfortable to you as well).

Let's assume the problem you are having is behaviour in a meeting. Notice I didn't say the problem was Bill. The problem was the behaviour in the meeting (remove the person as the identification of the problem). I perceived it to be condescending and my new strategy is that I'm not going to react at all. I'm not going to acknowledge what I consider to be rude and disrespectful behaviour. I'm going to pretend I didn't hear it. I'm just going to keep on going. After a couple of times, they're either going to get better or get worse in their behaviour because they're not getting the payoff they want, or the reaction from me they've become used to receiving. My strategy is to appear like it doesn't bother me at all, and that I choose not to be baited by their behaviour.

It takes at least five times to see how this strategy works. If the behavior is not *obviously* escalating, am I willing to stick a little longer to see what will happen? If it is diminishing, then I know it's working, so I'm definitely going to stick to this particular pattern. If it is escalating, am I willing to stick to the plan a little longer to see who reaches a boundary first? Am I at my boundary with their new behaviour? Do I need to do something different again?

You will have to wait to see which direction the behaviour is going and decide whether you are willing to accept the results, or whether you need to change something again.

But you have to be willing to do it five times, consistently, and therein lies the challenge. It may take you three months to get those five situations again. It depends on how much exposure you have to that person. Part of doing something different is to evaluate what you've done, try something new, evaluate it, try something new, evaluate it, but don't give up on it. Analyze the situation and think, "What did I do that maybe I shouldn't have done or what did I do that worked and I'm going to continue doing it?" Gauge your own behaviour and the reaction that it gets. It's tough. It takes a ton of effort. It is worth doing.

All this is easier to implement if you are clear on your strategy, and that is why you need to decide on your strategy right from the beginning. Strategy first, tactics second.

Can you get out of the way of this difficult behaviour? Is there something that you're doing that is actually causing the situation to escalate by our reaction, what we're saying, what we're doing, how we're internalizing it? It is definitely not an overnight fix. It's a very long-term solution. Naturally, it is worth it, but anything worth having isn't easy.

The length of the solution might also depend on how often you come in contact with this person. If it is someone who sits in the cubicle next to you, the situation could escalate faster and be resolved faster, however if it is someone you only see in a meeting every few months, it could take a year to resolve.

Of course, if you only see them every few months, it's potentially a situation you can live with, and hopefully not a big deal. If it is the person in the cubicle beside you, it is more critical.

Those are the situations that drive people to quit their jobs.

Statistically, 55% of people are not satisfied with their jobs

(SOURCE: I Can't Get No...Job Satisfaction, That Is: America's Unhappy Workers, Research Report #1459-09-RR, The Conference Board, 2013).

They stay in the jobs because they need the money and the security, but more important it is the people they work with that makes someone stay or leave. Enjoy or hate.

They could find a job that pays and has security in a different department or in a different company, but they stay in the jobs because of the people they work with. Many people, and I include myself in this category, have left really good jobs because of someone they worked with. It's the people that make your job worthwhile. So when you're working with someone who is very difficult, that can destroy a good job because you dread going to work everyday.

I'm often approached by people in my
audiences who are working with a difficult

person who happens to be their boss, and they wonder how they have to change their strategy in that situation.

In this situation you are probably going to be a little more passive in your approach, as opposed to aggressive. If the boss's payoff is control, it would be fairly stupid of me to try to take away that control — at least if I want to stay in my job. I have to figure out another way.

I will probably have to be willing to accept more, to move my boundaries back a little. I would tend to be more tolerant of his or her payoff needs because I feel threatened. I have a need for security and that need is higher than my need to push back against the boss's control. So I decide the boss can have control so that I can keep my job.

Now if I really can't stand letting the boss have the degree of control he or she wants, if I really can't live with that, then I need to find another job. So the strategy for dealing with any difficult person is the same strategy used with the boss, but because of the fear involved, it's probably going to be a more cautious version of the strategy.

Chapter 8: Working Closely with a Difficult Person

Don't laugh, but the next strategy you need is patience. Didn't know that was a strategy? Well, it is.

That means not blurting out the first thing that comes to mind when someone says something you don't like. And because you are sitting side-by-side with this person all day, every day, you need to be on your toes much more than with a co-worker from another department you see every few weeks at a meeting. You'll need more patience, and probably the ability to bite your tongue and not jump on every little issue you consider to be difficult behaviour.

In the case of not working closely with your difficult person, you can set yourself up before the meeting starts with self-talk statements such as: "I'm going to do x and y (your strategy), everything I planned. And I'm going to keep my mouth shut." You have your action plan ready and it's easier to implement it, because you are only having to deal with this person occasionally. This is good for family situations, the spouse of the friend you can't stand, and the person at work, from another department, that drives you crazy.

However, when you're working side by side with your difficult person, you can't do that all day long every day. Your willpower and your ability is just not strong enough to do that. You need a different strategy.

A useful approach is to break the day into segments and decide your strategy for each segment. From the morning to the first break, this is what I'm going to do. From the first break to lunch I'll do that. Or it may be the same thing four times a day.

Alcoholics Anonymous has a strategy of taking one day at a time, but dealing with difficult people every day is more like one hour at a time!

When you don't say exactly what is on your mind and when you stick to your strategy, you can reward yourself. The reward is up to you, but recognize that you have followed your plan and taken appropriate action. Then move on to the next segment of time.

Triggers and Hot Buttons

You have to be very aware of where the trigger buttons are when you're dealing with a difficult person, especially when you're working close to them. Many of those trigger buttons are language, so how you communicate with them on a day-to-day basis is vital.

Use *I* language as opposed to **you** language. For example, say things such as: *I want, I think, I feel, I hear, I need, I see*, as opposed to *you should, you need to, you have to, you must*. Those **you** statements are trigger buttons, and you don't want to trigger the other person or they will respond in kind and the situation will spiral out of control. Starting a statement with "You" (should/must/have to/need to) is the equivalent of Partner A pushing against Partner B. You didn't mean to cause tension, but you did, and they are likely to react the very same way as in our example.

If I say, "I need this done by 2:00 p.m.," I'm not as likely to trigger that other person as if I said, "You need to have this back to me by 2:00 p.m." I'm watching my language and my strategy is to avoid any tension, any trigger buttons. They still may not like that I need it by 2:00 pm but this language doesn't cause them to tense up and react to my "controlling" statement.

If it really is a very difficult situation, we're probably not in casual chitchatting mode anyway, and it's really a work-oriented discussion we're having. But even in casual chitchat I'm going to be aware of the difference between *I* language and **you** language. This means taking ownership, especially professionally, for what I need, I think, I want, I hear. It also means being aware that any time a sentence starts with the word 'you,' as in you need, you must, you have to, you should, it is likely to trigger a negative reaction. If things get bad enough, even a simple compliment like "You look nice today" brings a sharp retort like, "What do you mean by that?"

I'm going to be aware of how I communicate with my difficult person at all times. I'm going to be hypersensitive to what comes out of my mouth because I don't want to put the first spark on the embers of the fire. If I do that by using **you** language, they may see that as accusatory, and then they perceive me as being the difficult one.

Remember — they're probably not reading this book! They don't necessarily know these language nuances and they might well use the **you** language when they address you. It's important to hold yourself back from reacting when they say 'you need to.' After all, you do want to create some type of working relationship that you can manage. It isn't necessary to like everyone you work with, but it is necessary to be able to work with them.

However, if I'm working closely with you, I do need to be able to respect you. I might respect that you're just doing your job (even though it is a hindrance to me). I might respect you're a good parent. I might respect that you know a lot about X subject.

I would never ever go on the show "The Apprentice" because I do not like Donald Trump. I would need to give the guy a makeover in a hurry — a haircut at the very least, right? Seriously, I don't think I like Donald Trump. I don't want to have anything to do with him socially. However, I can also say that should I be sitting beside him on a flight one day, I would be able to carry on a conversation with him because I can respect that the man knows how to make money. It's not necessarily the way I want to make money, and he doesn't make the same decisions that I would have if I were running his company, but I respect he's done some major things that I can learn from. I could have that conversation with him and be respectful.

I have a friend who works with a woman he just can't stand. I don't think there's anything about her that he likes and he goes home every night and relays to his wife everything this woman has said or done that day.

The problem is that not only does not like the woman, but he doesn't respect her either. He doesn't respect her job. From his perspective, she doesn't work at all. He is actually unable to have a professional relationship with her because he neither likes her nor respects her.

Fortunately, they're just coworkers and they share the same space, but they don't really share a lot of the same work function, and they don't really work together. There's still a lot of tension with each other just because they're physically close.

If in some circumstance in the future he needed to work with her in a professional capacity, I would tell him he needs to find *something* that he respects about her. Why? Because he could inadvertently damage his own reputation by talking about her to others. "Did you see what *she* did today? I don't understand why she is in that position".

This is what typically happens, and I wonder if you have ever given in to this temptation. If so, you're potentially putting your reputation on the line because you're being a gossip. You're potentially being a bully without even realizing it.

You have to find respect for something about the person. Maybe just respect she's good at her job. I can talk to her about work. I don't need to care what she did on the weekend, and I'm not going to ask. Have some really clear conversational boundaries as well. Don't pretend you like this person when you really don't. Don't be rude, but don't pretend that you're buddies either.

By the way, those dislike relationships are always two-way. We all have someone in our lives we just can't stand — for any reason or for no reason! I know someone like that in my professional association. When I see him, I pretend I like him and he pretends he likes me, but we're both 100% clear we can't stand each other. From the outside, we're saying hello and on the inside we're both saying, "Get me out of here, get me out of here, get me out of here."

We pretend when we have to, but if we don't have to, we don't. He's not my friend on Facebook. He's not my friend on LinkedIn. I wouldn't go sit beside him at an event. We pretend, but we're not fooling each other at all.

Now in our society, a certain level of pretense is appropriate for the sake of civility, but don't over pretend. Say what you need to say and get out of the situation. Be polite and respectful at all times.

I do believe that if you are in a situation where you know you neither like nor respect your boss, you should get another job.

That to me really is a boundary. If there's nothing about your boss that you can respect, you are not even remotely doing yourself a favour by staying in that position because you're going to destroy your reputation by saying or doing something unprofessional. You're going to destroy your attitude.

Maybe you can't get another job today, but

you should be looking for another job because you're going to say something you'll never be able to take back. You don't have to like your boss, but you have to respect them in that you believe they can do their job.

Another strategy for working side by side is a little compassion. Put yourself in their shoes, take a look at your behaviour from their perspective. I'm not saying they are right, but in a crazy world, how would they perceive your behaviour? Whether you agree with her or not, it's good to look in the mirror sometimes just to see if you are really pushing buttons that you don't think you are.

It's a bit like that TV show "What Not to Wear." Have you ever watched that television program? If you don't know the show, it's about helping people who have no fashion common sense. They videotape people walking around town and then show them the video pointing out their clothing and asking them what they were thinking when they put that outfit on. They are genuinely surprised — and not in a good way! "Holy smokes, I had no idea I looked that bad," and we at home in the audience are asking, "Seriously? Because that looks really bad." You need to do the same kind of thing with your behaviour. Imagine that invisible camera is saying, "Okay, this is what it looks like. Are you aware that it looks like that?" That's self-reflection. It's really hard to do, but it can help us understand how we appear to the other person in the problem relationship.

When we are working side by side, we have to make sure that we are having conversations *with* our coworkers (not *at* our coworkers), just making sure that it's a two-way feedback style of communication, as opposed to just firing information and walking away.

Many people rely on email in difficult situations and that's not necessarily the best way to communicate. We know that, but everyone loves email in tension-filled situations, because we want the paper trail. If you ever have a difficult email to send, and if you've ever had to ask someone else, "How does this look? Does it look okay to you?" it doesn't. You could write "The sky is blue" and they'd read "THE SKY IS BLUE YOU IDIOT!", because the tone is added by the person reading the email. If you have tension in your relationship, the tone won't be the same way you intended it to be. Have more verbal conversations than email conversations, despite the temptation. Have more verbal conversations, be polite and civil and move forward, and definitely be flexible.

The world is not black and white. It's not about you're right and they're wrong. It's about degrees, so be flexible because there are different ways to see and do things. There are different boundaries. There are different rules on communication. I know you think your rules are right and they think their rules are right. Is there any room for flexibility, for compromise in this situation so you can make it through?

It's unreasonable to think that if you have a difficult person in your life that you're going to be best friends a week from now, a year from now, a hundred years from now. You're never going to be best friends. You do want to be able to get to the point where every day is not tension-filled, where you don't dread going into work, to where when you see that person you don't stiffen up. You want to get to the point where you can be civil and you can work and it doesn't keep you up at night. That's the goal. It's not the goal to be best friends. That's not going to happen.

Chapter 9: How to Respond When Someone Is Yelling At You

Situations where someone is yelling at you are definitely a challenge. It seems that no matter how well a strategy normally works, when an irate coworker or client happens it's in the here and now, and we all tend to just freeze. There's that sudden sinking feeling in the pit of our stomach and then panic sets in.

Customer Service is an area where this happens regularly, and if you're in that field you've probably become fairly good at handling these types of situations. You would have to learn, or you would leave your job, as the stress level would eat you alive.

However, if you work with someone who is prone to outbreaks of anger, you can work on your mindset so that you are ready when it happens. There are actually a few things you can do in this situation.

1. Stand up

Obviously you can't do this in every situation, but if you are able to stand up without causing an immediate surge of aggression, then stand up. If you are on the telephone, or even dealing with a virtual situation such as an exchange of nasty emails, stand up. Why? Because there is a better oxygen flow through your body when you stand and that changes your energy, makes it stronger. When you get oxygen to your brain you tend to think with a clearer mind, and you can stay on your strategic path. Lack of oxygen causes us to panic, and we react instead of respond to the situation. You also actually sound better too. Your voice is smoother, a little deeper and a little more confident when you are standing.

When you're sitting down, especially if they are standing in front of you, you are at a disadvantage. You are in an unfair power situation. It feels as if they're in a dominant position. You're sitting — you're trapped. If you can and it's not perceived as aggressive, stand up. Be careful though.

In a face-to-face meeting this is difficult to do, because it would probably be perceived as aggressive. If I'm on the phone the other person won't know I'm standing up but I'm getting the benefit of all that good oxygen supporting my brain, then I should stand up.

If I perceive that potentially this meeting might get difficult or contentious, perhaps I should just have the meeting standing, and never sit down at all. The other person likely wouldn't be sitting either, so we are on a fair playing field so to speak.

2. Bite your tongue (not literally, of course!)

When someone is yelling at you, the natural reaction for some is to yell back, for some it's to run away, for some it's to interrupt, and for some it's to cry.

None of these will work.

What you do want to do is bite your tongue and don't say a word. While they're venting, let them vent. There have actually been studies done on this that show the average vent of an angry person is 45 seconds long. That's a really long time. When somebody is letting you have it, telling you that you're incompetent or that you're stupid, that's a really long time to hear them. Normally at about the seven or eight-second mark, we interrupt them, and of course that's like a red rag to a bull. It makes the situation a lot worse. Bite your tongue and let them vent, and don't interrupt them. That's brutally difficult.

Think of it this way. When they are venting, they cannot hear you. All you can do is make them angrier. You cannot say anything that will calm them down in this situation. You could say "I'll give you a million dollars if you just stop talking right now" and they wouldn't have heard you. Don't waste your energy by trying to shorten the vent. You will only lengthen it. And, it is seen as disrespectful to interrupt (and perceived as you pushing on your partner). Don't push. Let them vent.

3. Breathe!

While you're biting your tongue and letting them vent, you should be reciting (silently) "Breathe in, breathe out, breathe in, breathe out." It's almost like a little meditation to get you to the end of the vent. You're hearing what they're saying, but you're not absorbing and you're not responding to every single thing they say. Don't allow the vent to become an argument. Arguments don't solve situations, they escalate them.

4. Maintain eye contact

While they're venting and you're purposely

concentrating on breathing in and out, you need to maintain eye contact while it is all happening. I know it is difficult, but it's essential.

If you look down at the floor, that looks as if you're being chastised. If you look up to the ceiling, that looks as if you're rolling your eyes. If you look away, that looks as if you're being dismissive.

Even though it's a challenge when someone is screaming at you, you do want to maintain eye contact. Here's a little trick to make it less uncomfortable for you.

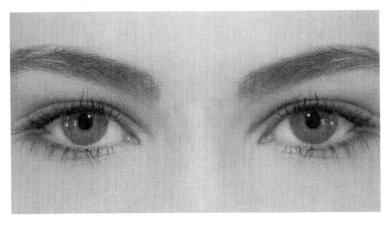

When you're really trying to hold it together, you're trying not to cry, you're trying not to yell, you're trying not to scream back, when you're trying to maintain eye contact with someone

78

and you're emotionally charged or you're having a tough time, here's what to do. Focus on a spot above the person's nose and between their eyebrows. If you look at that spot, they can't tell that you're not looking at their eyes, and it feels like eye contact to them. But it allows you to be a little detached.

The eyes are the windows to the soul. If you make direct, real eye contact with them when they're angry, you're going to pick up their anger. If they've got water in their eyes, you're going to want to cry. But looking at that spot between their eyebrows allows you to get a little bit detached and it still gives the impression that you're maintaining eye contact so that you can focus.

5. Don't tell them to calm down!

That's probably the worst thing you can ever say, especially when somebody is yelling at you and screaming. You want to let them get through their 45 second rant (average), even though in your head it feels like 45 minutes. When they're done, don't say, "Are you done?" Don't be sarcastic or condescending.

They're probably going to have a couple of starts and stops before they're done, but before you get to your turn to respond, take a deep breath and say something like, "I'm sorry you feel this way." or "I'm sorry this has happened." or "It's unfortunate it's come to this." Something slightly 'vanilla' that doesn't point fingers, that doesn't hit back. The anger is like an explosive inside and once it goes, it just goes. There's no point interrupting them or telling them to calm down.

Have you ever watched a Charlie Brown cartoon? The only adult on the Charlie Brown cartoon show is the teacher and you only ever hear the teacher go 'Wah wah wah'. You remember that sound? Well while they're venting, that's how you sound to them. There's no point in saying anything while they're venting. They need to get the venom out.

One of the best things that you can do here is ask a question and then stop talking. Ask a question such as, "Where else has this happened?" or "What do you think we can do to fix it?" It's some sort of innocuous question that keeps them going, so they're getting rid of the venom. Hopefully at this point, you are able to figure out what, out of all this tirade, you want to focus on. The one thing.

Telling them to calm down is not going to

allow you (or them) to focus on what the real issue is. It creates its own issue for you to deal with. It makes the other person skyrocket, and often become completely unreasonable.

6. Give feedback

You need to give some type of feedback to show that you've been listening.

You're going to do that using the *I* language we talked about earlier, to let them know you've heard what they were saying. But you're going to feedback one component of whatever all that venom was about — that's why you need to pick the one point to focus on.

Some people teach that you should say, "So, if I hear you correctly, you're saying. . ." I find that insulting because it's obvious that somebody learned that in a book. It's technique and I hate technique.

You do want to let them understand you've heard them, but in a very natural way. You might try some kind of feedback that says, "Okay so let's talk about...," or "Let's consider..." or "Let me defend X." But remember, just one component. They may have vented about ten different things. We are narrowing the focus to one.

Here's an important bit of bad news though: you don't get to vent back! It's not fair, I know, but you don't get a vent. Instead, you need to say something to calm the rough waters.

In customer service, for example, one of the lines I suggest is, "If that happened to me, I'd be upset, too." Notice, this doesn't actually mean you think it happened. It's a good line. You can add a second part, such as, "What can we do to fix it?" or "What can I do to make you happy?"

Make it sound like you and not some memorized technique you learned from a book. If you are sincere, that will come across. If you are memorizing a technique, that will show as well.

What you're doing here is calming the angered person down (without telling them to do so). You want to find out from them exactly what they want. What are they looking for? One of the best ways to find out what they want is to just flat out ask them. "What can I do to fix this?"

Interestingly, most of the time, it's nothing!

They just wanted to vent. If you ask them this question and they answer, "Nothing!", just reply, "Okay" and hopefully the venting situation is over and you can both move on.

Now I hear you asking, but what if they're standing at my desk? That calls for a variation on the same solution. This time you say, "Okay, maybe we could talk about this later." or "Maybe you want to postpone this to another time." or "Do you want to touch base on this again next week? Or do you want to leave it alone for now or come back to it?'

The reality is that once they say "Nothing!" they'll probably just walk away anyway and it's over Of course it's not really over. It's just simmering, and it could break out again at any moment. I would then go up to them a little later on and say, "Look, I was uncomfortable with the conversation we had about an hour ago. Do you think we can talk about that?" or "I need to get something off my chest."

Don't try this while they are yelling. The goal in the moment is to let them get it out of their system. Actually, it's really important that they get it out, so be willing to put your needs on hold for a bit because if you don't deal with their anger, you're wasting your time. They are just going to get angrier.

You need to bring the anger down so that you can get to a point where there is a solution, where there is a move forward point and then do that. If you need to, come back and visit the issue later on.

Anger is contagious, and the last thing you want to do is fight back with anger as well. Your goal is not to get angry at them. The goal is to bring the emotional temperature right down. Is it in your best interest to stand your ground, or is it in your best interest to get the anger situation resolved right now and then talk about the real issue later when emotions are much calmer? It's really best to get the anger fixed right now and deal with the issue later because right now, neither you nor the other person is working with the rational brain.

This is not about giving into what they need. It's about de-escalating the situation and then trying to fix the problem at a more rational time later so that it doesn't happen again.

Calm it down. Deal with the confrontation required separately (see next Chapter).

How to Let Someone Know They Are Being Difficult

It really takes a strong person to be willing to do this, but if you are strong enough and have decided to do it, you need to work on doing it properly.

After the situation and major tension has passed, go to your person a little later on and say, "I want to talk about X." Use all the *I* language we've talked about and focus on the facts. In other words, stay away from judgment statements and just state the facts.

So, for example, you might say, "Yesterday in our group meeting, I felt very uncomfortable when it was pointed out that I was late for the meeting." Notice, I'm not saying they pointed a finger at me. I'm not using *you* language. I'm not blaming that person.

No matter how difficult it may feel, you've got to stop talking. Don't say another word. Again, it's not your turn to vent. That's not how you're going to let somebody know that they're difficult.

They might say, "Oh, well, I don't know why that bothered you." You then say, "It did."

You know, you really need to say so very little, but it needs to be in the right words with the right intent.

Never accuse someone directly of being a difficult person. Don't say, "I want to let you know that yesterday at the meeting you were being very difficult," because that's your perception. Don't accuse someone of having a bad attitude or being condescending or anything else that is your perception. They don't know what you mean, so how can they fix it? Talk about facts, and things that are measurable.

"I noticed in yesterday's meeting that you never referred to me by name. You called me 'hey you' and that bothers me." Talk about specifics and explain to them how it makes you feel. "From my perspective, it looks as if you don't respect what I do in the workplace."

Talking about how you feel gives them permission to say, "Well, that's not true." That's okay, but at least you brought it to their attention. You're not going to get them to agree, "Oh, yeah. I've been a real jerk." You're never going to get that out of anyone (especially when they think that *you're* the one being difficult or being a jerk), but you might make them actually think about their behaviour in a different light.

Don't tell people they are being difficult, because they will probably reply that they're not being difficult, and that you are. Instead, tell them a problem you are having and what you've done about it and ask for their help. Here's what I mean:

"I want to talk to you about a challenge I've been having with feeling respected here at work. I'm wondering if you can help me." Say that, and then just stop talking. I mean *stop talking* and wait for their response. You will have a temptation to fill in the silence. Don't.

This might result in a conversation like this:

> You: All my mistakes are being constantly pointed out, and it makes me feel as if I'm not qualified to do this job, even though I know I am. (Notice I didn't accuse the other person of being the one to be the problem. I didn't say "You constantly are pointing out my mistakes").
>
> Other: That's not why I pointed your mistakes out.
>
> You: But that's what it feels like to me.
>
> Other: I'm doing it to help you so you can be better at your job.
>
> You: But I feel as if I'm being set up to be fired.

This, of course, is a very uncomfortable conversation, but it does give them an insight into how things look from your perspective. It doesn't guarantee it will change, but it hopefully gives you both a different perspective and perhaps in the future the behavior will be different.

Dealing with Difficult People

Chapter 10: How to Recognize a Successful Strategy

As I mentioned earlier, you should expect to see their behaviour get worse before it gets better. As you start to change your behaviour at first you're going to shock your difficult person. They're saying to themselves, "Wait a second, somebody just changed the rules to the game," and they didn't even know there was a game. When Partner A pushes, they're expecting Partner B to push back. That's the natural reaction. When Partner B doesn't push back, Partner A is almost shocked into pulling back.

Remember, you're not necessarily trying to take away the other person's payoff; you just want to change behaviour.

If the chronically negative person says, "Oh no, it's snowing. It's April. I can't believe it's snowing in April," you might say something like, "You know what? The farmers appreciate all the water. We're going to have some good vegetables this year." They're going to look at you and think, "Hmm." You didn't spew back more negativity, but you answered, so they got the payoff they wanted — attention — and of course that took the tension away so there's nothing left for them to push against.

They're not looking to fight with you. Their behaviour might start to change gradually. The next day they come into work and say, "So, Helen, it's snowing out today. You must be really happy." It's not exactly the positivity you want, but it's not entirely negative. Remember, they're confused because you changed the game.

But after a few times the behaviour will either become more difficult or it will dissipate a little. If it dissipates, you'll know your strategy is working. If the behaviour gets worse after five times or so, then it's clearly not working so you need to try a different strategy.

When tension does lessen, it's because you've just simply gotten out of the way. They perceive you as not being difficult any more, and you're seeing the same thing in them. What happened here? You both backed off without realizing it!

This is the goal: get the relationship to a point where it's not tension-filled all the time. It may not be loving, but it's not stress-filled. So keep trying until you get there.

Closing Thoughts

In any situation where there's a difficult person relationship, you have to ask yourself if it's worth doing the work to change it. Just because someone is annoying you or just because there's tension in the relationship doesn't mean this is your battle to fight. There are some things that you need to just let go.

It may bug me that my dad needs his grass cut at a 45-degree angle because I think that that's a waste of time and energy. But it's important to him, and my relationship with him is more important to me than the grass, so I will cut the grass the way he wants it.

My relationship with my co-worker is important to me. So even though she feels a competitive need to point out everything I do wrong, my relationship with her is more important than my need to be perfect, so I'm not going to fight back or I'm not going to point out her mistakes.

I care very much about the correct use of the language and grammar, so I want to correct people's emails and Facebook posts! It really bothers me to see the language destroyed, but I don't edit their messages because my reputation is important and I don't want to come across as difficult.

Sometimes you just value the relationship more than being right. And so you let it go.

If you are in a situation where you need to deal with a difficult person, first ask yourself if it's worth doing anything about it. If you decide it is, I hope the advice in this book will help you release the tension and arrive at a relationship both you and the other person can, at least, live with and, at best, enjoy.

Worksheets

Your Strategy

☐ What is the behavior

☐ Why are they doing this (payoff)

☐ Is it innocent or intentional

☐ How do they see your behavior

☐ What can you I differently to get a different reaction

☐ Create tactics to follow

☐ Evaluate after 5 attempts

☐ Continue same tactic, or create another

> I would be more effective
> working with _____
>
> If _____.

My targets for Change

1) The System
2) The Other Person
3) Me!!!

Plan A

> ### List of things that I can possibly do to get a different reaction from my difficult person
>
> •
>
> •
>
> •
>
> •
>
> •
>
> •
>
> •
>
> ### Which one will I try first (remember, five times before choosing another option)?